The Treaty of Versailles, 1919

A Primary Source Examination of the Treaty That Ended World War I

૭๏ ૭๏ ૭๏

Corona Brezina

rosen central
Primary Source™

The Rosen Publishing Group, Inc., New York

Fait à Versailles, le vingt-huit un mil neuf cent dix-neuf, en un seul exemplaire qui restera déposé dans les archives du Gou-

Done at Versailles, the twenty-eighth day of june, one thousand nine hundred and nineteen, in a single copy which will remain

Published in 2006 by The Rosen Publishing Group, Inc.
29 East 21st Street, New York, NY 10010

Library of Congress Cataloging-in-Publication Data

Brezina, Corona.
The Treaty of Versailles, 1919: a primary source examination of the treaty that ended World War I/by Corona Brezina.—1st ed.
    p. cm.—(Primary sources of American treaties)
Includes bibliographical references.
ISBN 1-4042-0442-3 (library binding)
1. World War, 1914–1918—Peace. 2. Paris Peace Conference (1919–1920) 3. Treaty of Versailles (1919) 4. World War, 1914–1918—Peace—Sources. 5. Treaty of Versailles (1919)—Sources. I. Title. II. Series.
D644.B82 2006
940.3'141—dc22

                                                    2004030622

Manufactured in the United States of America

On the cover: *(From left to right)* French prime minister Georges Clemenceau, American president Woodrow Wilson, and British prime minister David Lloyd George acknowledge an appreciative crowd in Versailles, France, after signing the Treaty of Versailles on June 28, 1919.

Contents

Introduction

The First World War (1914–1918) was the most horrific conflict the world had ever experienced. The war
introduced new weapons and new fighting techniques.
For the first time in history, soldiers faced tanks, combat
aircraft, powerful machine guns, submarines, and chemical
weapons on the battlefield. Troops huddled in trenches as the
conflict dragged on for months and years of near deadlock. The
world's first large-scale genocide—Turkey's killing of 1.5
million Armenians—occurred during the war. By the time the
war ended, over 9 million men had died on the battlefield.

The war began in 1914 with the assassination of an
Austro-Hungarian nobleman. At the end of the war, the Austro-
Hungarian Empire had fallen. Three other great empires also
collapsed during World War I: the czarist regime of Russia,
the German Empire, and the Ottoman Empire of Turkey.

On November 11, 1918, an armistice ended the fighting.
In London, Paris, and the other Allied capitals of Europe,
people thronged the streets in celebration. Guns were fired
to mark the hour of the cease-fire. Their jubilation did not
last long. It was quieted by the reality that Europe had been
devastated by four years of bloodshed and destruction.

Parisians gather around the Statue of Strasbourg in Paris, France, on November 11, 1918, to celebrate news of the armistice. The happy crowd has decorated the statue with flags and flowers. The statue previously had been covered with a black shroud to mourn the city of Strasbourg being under German control since 1871.

"We have won the war . . . now we have to win the peace," declared French prime minister Georges Clemenceau at the Paris Peace Conference, where leaders from France and other victorious nations assembled in early 1919. For nearly six months, they worked to draft a peace settlement they hoped would bring stability to Europe and prevent the recurrence of war. The result was the Treaty of Versailles.

It was an ambitious and optimistic effort that ended in failure. The delegates who drafted the terms of the Treaty of Versailles could never have anticipated the economic and political turmoil that swept through Europe during the 1920s. The treaty was ineffective in its mission to create a peaceful world in which countries would never again have to resort to war. Ultimately, the flawed Treaty of Versailles contributed to the conditions that led to World War II.

Fait a Versailles, le vingt-huit juin mil neuf cent dix-neuf, en un seul exemplaire qui restera déposé dans les archives du Gouvernement de la République française et dont les expeditions authen—

Done at Versailles, the twenty-eighth day of June, one thousand nine hundred and nineteen, in a single copy which will remain deposited in the archives of the French Republic, and of which

"The War to End All Wars"

It was December 1918, and American president Woodrow Wilson was receiving a hero's welcome in Paris. Cheering crowds thronged to see him as he toured French landmarks such as the Arc de Triomphe and the Avenue des Champs-Elysées. Buildings flew French and American flags, flowers rained down on Wilson's carriage, and airplanes roared overhead. He could hear the drums of a mounted band in the background.

President Wilson had recently arrived in France for the Paris Peace Conference. He made history by becoming the first American president to travel abroad while in office. But these were historic times. The Allies (Britain, France, Italy, the United States, and twenty-three other nations) had just won World War I, defeating the Central Powers of Germany, Austria-Hungary, Bulgaria, and Turkey. Now the victors were assembling in Paris to draft the peace settlement. The decisions made by the statesmen at the conference would have a profound impact on how Europe would restore order after the widescale death and devastation caused by World War I.

This photograph shows French troops coming under German fire during the Battle of Verdun, one of the costliest engagements of World War I. The Battle of Verdun lasted for ten months and caused more than 700,000 casualties, which includes soldiers killed, wounded, or missing.

⧽ The Roots of the War ⧽

At the time, World War I was dubbed "the war to end all wars," reflecting the belief that humanity would never again see such a horrific conflict. The war shattered Europe. The men who gathered for the Paris Peace Conference faced a greater task than the negotiation of a treaty with a defeated enemy. In order to secure a lasting peace, they had to resolve the issues that had caused World War I in the first place.

On the eve of the war, what were known as the Great Powers—Germany, Austria-Hungary, Italy, Russia, France, and Great Britain—dominated Europe. These countries vied against each other for economic and military supremacy. Most of them adopted compulsory military service for young men and maintained large standing armies in case of war. Britain and Germany competed for dominance of the seas by building up fleets of battleships. In addition, the Great

Powers were engaged in a race for colonies, especially in Africa and Asia. By controlling territory beyond their borders, their leaders sought to transform their countries into global powers. During the decades before World War I, the Great Powers competed and occasionally fought over colonies.

Europe maintained a balance of power through a complicated system of alliances. These agreements were sometimes negotiated and signed in secret. By 1914, the Great Powers were split between two rival alliance systems. Germany, Austria-Hungary, and Italy made up the Triple Alliance. However, Italy could no longer be counted on to support its allies. The Triple Alliance was opposed by the Triple Entente, which consisted of Britain, France, and Russia.

Bordered by Russia on the east and France on the west, Germany was positioned between two potentially hostile neighbors. German military officers envisioned the possibilities of enemy armies attacking from either side.

The tense situation was made worse by ethnic strife between and within the Great Powers, especially in Central and Eastern Europe. During the nineteenth century, a wave of nationalistic pride swept across Europe. Many Europeans belonged to ethnic groups that shared common languages, cultural traditions, and histories, but did not possess national sovereignty. Poland, for example, had been divided among Russia, Prussia (part of present-day Germany), and Austria. The Austro-Hungarian government in particular ruled a number of ethnic minorities within its empire. Sixty percent of its population were Slavs—Bosnians, Czechs, Montenegrins, Poles, Serbs, and Slovaks— who had no voice in the

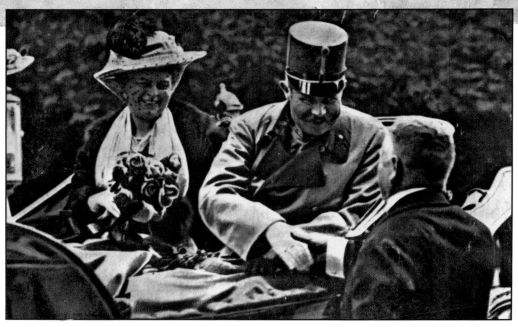

Archduke Francis Ferdinand of Austria and his wife, Countess Sophie, ride in an open carriage during a motorcade in Sarajevo, Bosnia, on June 28, 1914, hours before they were assassinated by Gavrilo Princip. The assassination was planned by the Black Hand, a Serbian terrorist organization, to protest Austria's 1908 annexation of Bosnia and to thwart the archduke's plan to further integrate Bosnia into the Austro-Hungarian Empire.

empire's government. In 1908, Austria-Hungary annexed the province of Bosnia on the Balkan Peninsula, home to many ethnic Serbs. The Serbs felt greater loyalty to the small kingdom of Serbia across the border than to Austria-Hungary. Russia considered itself a patron and protector of Serbia and other Slavs in the Balkans.

On June 28, 1914, Gavrilo Princip, a young Bosnian Serb nationalist, assassinated Archduke Francis Ferdinand, an Austrian nobleman. The regional dispute that followed quickly grew into an international war.

The empire of Austria-Hungary held the Serbian government responsible for the attack, despite a lack of proof. On July 23, Austria-Hungary issued an ultimatum to Serbia. If Serbia did not agree to its terms, Austria-Hungary would authorize war. Although Serbia accepted almost all of the demands, Austria-Hungary broke off diplomatic relations and declared war on July 28.

Russia reacted by mobilizing its military forces in preparation for war. In response, Germany sent out demands that Russia cease its mobilization and that France officially declare neutrality. These ultimatums were ignored. Germany immediately began mobilization, declared war on Russia and France, and invaded the neutral country of Belgium. On August 4, Great Britain declared war on Germany. The Allies—Britain, France, and Russia—prepared to march against Germany and Austria-Hungary, the Central Powers. The Ottoman Empire, or Turkey, joined the Central Powers. Italy and Japan sided with the Allies.

Every nation involved expected a quick and decisive war. But after the initial attacks, the struggle quickly reached a deadlock. Instead of advancing, troops began digging in. Both sides dug elaborate fortified trenches along the western front, which stretched for hundreds of miles from the French-Belgian border in the north down to Switzerland. Trench warfare between enemy lines lasted almost four years. Meanwhile, Russian forces fared badly against the Germans on the eastern front on Russia's border with Germany. In 1917, the czarist government of Russia collapsed. The new regime withdrew from the war and signed a treaty with Germany in 1918.

⁓ Woodrow Wilson's Fourteen Points ⁓

Upon the outbreak of the war, one of the world's most powerful countries remained neutral. The United States saw no reason to involve itself in a European conflict 2,000 miles (3,219 kilometers) away. In August 1914, former U.S. president William Taft published an article in *Independent* magazine, urging the country to stay neutral in the war. "We shall be suffering with the rest of the world, except that we shall not be destroying or blowing up our existing wealth or sacrificing the lives of our best young men and youth . . . The influence of America can be thrown most effectively for peace," he declared. President Woodrow Wilson, a Democrat, ran for reelection in 1916. He won with the campaign motto, "He kept us out of the war."

As the war stretched into months and years, Wilson attempted several times to mediate a peace agreement in Europe. He sent presidential adviser Colonel Edward M. House to Europe to initiate diplomatic steps toward a resolution, but with no success.

The war affected life in the United States despite American neutrality. At sea, German submarines battled Britain's powerful navy. Germany also attacked merchant and passenger ships carrying Americans, provoking outrage in the United States. In response, Germany limited its submarine warfare for a period. In February 1917, however, Germany escalated its submarine warfare against all ships, including American vessels, sailing near Britain. Two months later, Wilson asked Congress to declare war on Germany. "Armed neutrality, it now appears, is impracticable," he stated. "We are glad . . . to fight thus for the ultimate peace of the world and for the liberation of its peoples, the German peoples included." During the summer of 1917, the United States began shipping troops to Europe.

As evidenced by the slogans "Who keeps us out of war?" and "Peace with honor," President Woodrow Wilson emphasized his decision to keep the United States out of World War I in his reelection bid in 1916. Months after winning the election, Wilson ordered American troops to join the conflict.

On January 8, 1918, Wilson delivered a speech to Congress in which he laid out his Fourteen Points, a proposed program to end the war and establish world peace. It was an idealistic and ambitious plan. "What we demand in this war, therefore, is nothing peculiar [unique] to ourselves," Wilson stated. "It is that the world be made fit and safe to live in; and particularly that it be made safe for every peace-loving nation which, like our own, wishes to live its own life, determine its own institutions, be assured of justice and fair dealing by the other peoples of the world as against force and selfish aggression."

The first five points called for reforms in various issues of international concern. Secret diplomacy would cease—all negotiations and treaty-making would be conducted publicly.

Sixty-fifth Congress of the United States of America;

At the First Session,

Begun and held at the City of Washington on Monday, the second day of April, one thousand nine hundred and seventeen.

JOINT RESOLUTION

Declaring that a state of war exists between the Imperial German Government and the Government and the people of the United States and making provision to prosecute the same.

Whereas the Imperial German Government has committed repeated acts of war against the Government and the people of the United States of America: Therefore be it

Resolved by the Senate and House of Representatives of the United States of America in Congress assembled, That the state of war between the United States and the Imperial German Government which has thus been thrust upon the United States is hereby formally declared; and that the President be, and he is hereby, authorized and directed to employ the entire naval and military forces of the United States and the resources of the Government to carry on war against the Imperial German Government; and to bring the conflict to a successful termination all of the resources of the country are hereby pledged by the Congress of the United States.

Champ Clark

Speaker of the House of Representatives.

Thos. R. Marshall

Vice President of the United States and President of the Senate.

Approved 6. April, 1917.

Woodrow Wilson

This is the official congressional declaration of war on Germany in 1917, authorizing the United States' entry into World War I. It was signed by House Speaker Champ Clark, Vice President Thomas Marshall, and President Woodrow Wilson, on April 6.

There would be freedom of navigation on the seas. There would be free trade among nations. Nations would reduce their armaments. Powers that held colonies would agree to an "impartial adjustment of all colonial claims" that took into consideration the interests of the colonists.

The next eight points dealt with specific nations and national groups. Foreign troops would evacuate Russia, Belgium, and France. Russia's rights as a sovereign nation would be respected. Belgium, France, and Italy would have land restored to them. There would be a prospect of autonomy for the peoples of Austria-Hungary. There would also be a prospect of autonomy for non-Turkish members of the Ottoman Empire, and Turkey itself would be a sovereign nation. Poland would be established as an independent country.

Wilson's final point stated that "A general association of nations must be formed under specific covenants for the purpose of affording mutual guarantees of political independence and territorial integrity to great and small states alike." This proposed organization would later be called the League of Nations. Wilson envisioned the League of Nations as a body of democracies that would arbitrate disputes between countries before they resorted to war.

The Fourteen Points did not directly mention German aggression. Wilson ended the speech by urging the Germans to accept a just peace settlement. "We have no jealousy of German greatness, and there is nothing in this program that impairs it . . . We do not wish to fight her either with arms or with hostile arrangements of trade if she is willing to associate herself with us and other peace-loving nations of the world." Most of the nations involved in the war applauded Wilson's speech, but the Allies had reservations about his leniency toward Germany. France, Britain, Italy, and many smaller Allied nations blamed Germany for the war. They believed that Germany should pay for the bloodshed and devastation that the war had caused. Wilson elaborated on his Fourteen Points proposal in the subsequent eight months, adding the Four Principles, the Four Ends, and the Five Particulars.

Wilson's proposal did not bring an end to the fighting. But in 1918, the Allies began to advance against the Germans. With American support, the Allies had no shortage of men and weaponry. The Germans were running low on resources, and morale among the troops was low. Moreover, Germany seemed to be on the brink of a revolution from within. German leaders realized they had no hope of winning the war.

The U.S. Army's 61st Infantry arrived in Brest, France, in early 1918. Approximately 4,355,000 American soldiers were called into action during World War I. There were more than 364,800 casualties, including 126,000 deaths.

On October 4, 1918, Germany contacted the United States to request an armistice. Germany was willing to accept a peace settlement based on the Fourteen Points. Before negotiating peace terms, Wilson demanded that Germany cease its submarine warfare. He also sought proof that Germany was truly dedicated to creating a democratic state. On November 9, 1918, Kaiser Wilhelm II, the emperor of Germany, went into exile in the Netherlands. He agreed to abdicate his rule due to turmoil within Germany, not in response to Allied demands. A Socialist leader, Friedrich Ebert, took office as the chancellor and Germany was declared a republic.

Before beginning negotiations with the German armistice commission, Wilson asked the Allies to accept his Fourteen

Points. David Lloyd George, the prime minister of Britain, rejected the point concerning freedom of the seas. The Allies also demanded "compensation . . . for damage done to civilian population . . . and their property by the aggression of Germany."

On November 11, members of the German armistice commission and Allied representatives finalized the terms of the armistice. They signed the document on a railway car in French-controlled territory. The armistice officially ended all fighting of World War I.

Even in Wilson's hour of triumph on the world stage, he suffered a defeat at home. During the 1918 Senate races, Wilson had campaigned for fellow Democrats. He claimed that the Republicans had not fully supported him throughout the war. Wilson's accusation rallied the Republicans against him. In the November elections, Republicans gained a majority in the Senate. This meant that during negotiations for a permanent peace settlement, Wilson's political adversaries would control the U.S. Senate Committee on Foreign Relations, the congressional body that determined key aspects of international affairs.

⇌ Preparing for Peace ⇌

During the two months following the armistice, the leaders of the Allied countries planned the details of the upcoming peace conference. They haggled about when and where it should be held, who should attend, and how it should be organized. Wilson and Lloyd George wanted it to take place in neutral Switzerland. However, they finally agreed that

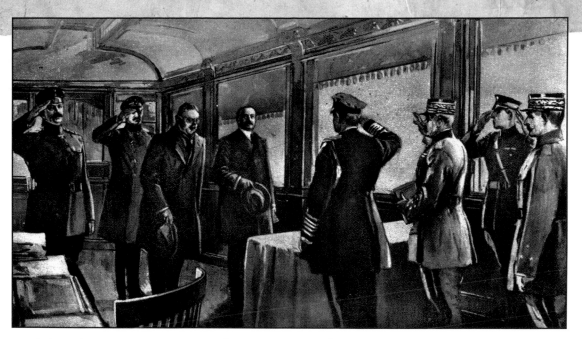

This drawing depicts the first meeting of Allied and German delegates to establish conditions for a conference to negotiate an armistice. The meeting took place in a railroad car in Rethondes, France. The artist was commissioned by the French government specifically to re-create the scene.

Paris, France, was a more practical location. Also, France had seen the worst of the fighting during the war. French prime minister Georges Clemenceau would preside as president of the conference. The plan of procedure would be agreed on after the conference began.

Germany was not invited to the conference. The Germans would not be given a voice in the negotiation of the peace settlement. After the Allies drew up the terms of a treaty, they would present it to Germany for ratification, or approval.

Fait a Versailles, le vingt-huit   Done at Versailles, the twenty
juin mil neuf cent dix neuf, en   eighth day of june, one thousand
un seul exemplaire qui restera   nine hundred and nineteen, in
déposé dans les archives du Gou-   single copy which will remain
vernement de la République fran-   deposited in the archives of th
caise et dont les expeditions authen   French Republic, and of which

The Paris Peace Conference

oung British delegate Harold Nicolson famously compared the atmosphere at the Paris Peace Conference to "that sense of riot in a parrot house." The proceedings were plagued by poor organization, poor communication, and an overwhelming amount of complex detail. As quoted in *The Versaille Settlement* by Alan Sharp, French diplomat Paul Cambon described the scene in frustration: "No matter how hard you try, you cannot imagine the shambles, the chaos, the incoherence, the ignorance here. Nobody knows anything because everything is happening behind the scenes."

Even before the conference began, Europeans began voicing complaints about the delay. Governments and national boundaries were in limbo. Families in war-torn areas had no food or money. The Allies, whose forces were already demobilizing, risked losing their power over Germany if the negotiations dragged on too long.

⟟ Visions of a Postwar Europe ⟟

The first session of the Paris Peace Conference opened on January 18, 1919. Leaders and representatives of thirty-two

The four main players at the Paris Peace Conference were (seated left to right) Prime Minister Vittorio Orlando of Italy, Prime Minister David Lloyd George of Britain, Prime Minister Georges Clemenceau of France, and President Woodrow Wilson of the United States.

countries had come to Paris, bringing with them thousands of delegates, expert advisers, and other aides. Hundreds of journalists also thronged to the site of the conference.

The Plenary Conference—the full assembly of delegates from every nation represented—met only eight times during the conference. It was quickly decided that a Council of Ten would be the primary forum for discussion and decision making. The Council of Ten consisted of two high-ranking delegates from each of the five main powers in attendance. The United States was represented by Wilson and Secretary of State Robert Lansing; France, by Clemenceau and Foreign Minister Stéphen Pichon; Britain, by David Lloyd George and Foreign Secretary Arthur Balfour; Italy, by Prime Minister Vittorio Orlando and Foreign Minister Sidney Sonnino; and Japan, by Baron Keishiro Matsui and Viscount Chinda (later by Prince Saionji and Baron Makino).

David Lloyd George was a highly respected lawyer before he first ran for political office in 1890. After twenty-six years in Parliament, he became prime minister of Britain in 1916, and served until 1922, when he resigned. Despite his significant role in drafting the Treaty of Versailles, he eventually considered it a failure.

Each of the Allied powers had different goals and expectations as the conference commenced. This frequently led to heated discussions. At least on one occasion, debates between Clemenceau and Lloyd George nearly resulted in blows; on another, Orlando dissolved into tears.

Georges Clemenceau was fiercely and passionately dedicated to ensuring France's future security. Like many of his countrymen, he wanted to see Germany crushed, both to punish the Germans for the war and to prevent any possibility of future aggression. Clemenceau wanted to seize some of Germany's territory and impose harsh reparation payments. He dreamed of neutralizing Germany by splitting it into three independent republics. Nicknamed the Tiger for his ferocious aggression and cutting tongue, he was a formidable defender of France's interests. Clemenceau frequently clashed with Wilson, whose idealistic and conciliatory proposals he considered ineffective. "How can I talk to a fellow who thinks himself the first man in two thousand years who has known anything about peace on earth?" he exclaimed in one frustrated moment, as quoted in *Woodrow Wilson and the Lost Peace*.

Lloyd George steered a middle course between Clemenceau's demands and Wilson's Fourteen Points. France and Britain were old rivals, and Lloyd George intended to thwart France's attempt to establish itself as the dominant European power. He wanted the German fleet neutralized so that Britain would once again be the greatest naval power in the world. He wanted Germany's colonial empire dissolved, preferably ceding some of its territorial possessions to Britain. But Lloyd George recognized that at some time in the future, Europe would have to reconcile with Germany. He wanted to impose some reparations on Germany, but not under terms so harsh that Germany's economy would collapse. If Germany was ruined, the entire European economy would suffer. At the same time, though, Lloyd George was a politician accountable to British voters. During the December 1918 election, British politicians demanded that harsh reparations be imposed on Germany. Politically, Lloyd George could not afford to be too lenient with Germany.

Wilson's first priority at the conference was the establishment of the League of Nations. Once the League came into force, he believed, it could resolve many of the other pressing issues facing Europe. When he arrived in Paris, Wilson realized that the European situation was far more complex than he had known when he drafted his peace proposal. Wilson liked having a firm grip on the facts on both sides of the issue before coming to a decision. In Paris, this was an impossible feat. Wilson often found himself outmatched in discussions. Both Clemenceau and Lloyd George were adept negotiators, honed by years of experience in rough-and-tumble European

This French World War I poster captures the distrust and animosity that the French people harbored against the Germans during the war. It shows a German man as both a salesman and a soldier carrying a torch and a bloody knife.

politics. Wilson's Fourteen Points were often vague enough to be interpreted in the Allies' favor. Even Wilson recognized that the Fourteen Points offered no clear resolution to some issues. For example, Italy claimed the city of Fiume near the Yugoslavian border, home of 30,000 Italians. "Signor Orlando," Wilson responded to the demand, "There are at least a million Italians in New York, but I trust that you will not on this score claim our Empire City as Italian territory," as quoted in Charles L. Mee's *The End of Order: Versailles, 1919.*

Neither the Italians nor the Japanese had much at stake in the League of Nations, reparations, or the fate of Germany. Their main concern was the distribution of territory. In return for Italian support, Britain had promised Italy part of the region of Dalmatia and some other territories. Similarly, France, Britain, and Italy had agreed to give Shandong, a German province in China, to Japan.

Delegates from the other nations represented at Paris were invited to attend only those sessions that affected their specific interests. These included Belgium, Canada, China, the Czechoslovak Republic, Hedjaz (Saudi Arabia), India, Poland, Romania, Serbia, Siam, and others. Ignaz Paderewski, renowned as a concert pianist as well as a statesman, represented Poland. One of the Czechoslovakian delegates was Foreign Minister Eduard Benes, who would later become president of Czechoslovakia.

⁓ The Peacemaking Process ⁓

The Council of Ten began by organizing a procedure and establishing commissions of experts to address specific items. These commissions focused on issues such as reparations and war crimes, international labor legislation, economics, and aviation. Later, territorial commissions were established to evaluate the claims of various lesser powers. In all, fifty-eight separate committees were established. While most of these eventually saw the results of their efforts included in the final treaty, the work of some commissions was neglected in the disorganization of the conference. The lesser Allies participated in discussions and consulted with these commissions while the Council of Ten attended to the most pressing issues.

The first major issue addressed at the conference was the Covenant of the League of Nations. Wilson himself presided over the commission in charge of drawing up the first draft. He insisted that the covenant be included in the final peace treaty rather than as a separate document. In Wilson's vision, the League would promote international peace through

This famous World War I painting by Sir William Orpen shows a meeting of the Council of Ten in the opulent Hall of Clocks at the Quai d'Orsay, Paris, France, in 1919. The Council of Ten consisted of the leaders and foreign ministers of the five main powers at the Paris Peace Conference.

arbitration. He resisted France's demands that the League maintain a standing army. Wilson wanted the League to move beyond the old system of military alliances and threats backed up by force. The commission also rejected a Japanese proposal to expand a call for "religious equality" to "religious and racial equality."

Wilson presented the covenant to the plenary session of the conference on February 14. Most delegates reacted with approval and enthusiasm. It was Wilson's greatest triumph of the conference.

During the opening weeks of the conference, the council set up the "mandate system" to deal with former German and Turkish colonies. Wilson agreed that Germany should be stripped of its colonies in Africa and Asia. However, he objected to the colonies being claimed outright by the victors. Meanwhile, South Africa, New Zealand, and Australia all wished to take possession of neighboring territory lost by the Germans. After negotiations, it was agreed that the former colonies—now called mandates—would be generally supervised by the League of Nations. Each mandate would be put under the direct administration of a "mandatory power" that would act as its guardian.

The Council of Ten spent many of its sessions in late January and early February listening to the claims of the smaller powers. Diplomatically, these minor powers deserved an opportunity to present their cases, but it was not a productive use of time for the council. According to Charles L. Mee in *The End of Order: Versailles, 1919*, Isaiah Bowman, an adviser to Wilson, described two such sessions: "When [Roman] Dmowski related the claims of Poland, he began at eleven o'clock in the morning and in the four- teenth century, and could only reach 1919 and the pressing problems of the moment only as late as four o'clock in the afternoon. [Eduard] Benes followed immediately after- wards with the counter claims of Czechoslovakia, and, if I remember correctly, he began a century earlier and finished an hour later."

In addition to their roles as peacemakers at the conference, the members of the Council of Ten served as the Supreme Council of the Allies. The Supreme Council essentially acted as an interim government for much of Europe until the Paris Peace Conference finished its work. The council established commissions such as the Supreme Economic Council to focus on specific aspects of administering European affairs. The Supreme Economic Council was so efficiently run that it became one of the most important international bodies in relieving the desperate plight of war-torn Europe.

The leaders of the Council of Ten also had to attend to the domestic affairs of their own countries during their time in Paris. Lloyd George made occasional trips back to London. On February 15, Wilson departed to spend a month in Washington. He met with Republican Senate leaders who were hostile to the League of Nations and Wilson's other plans for Europe, but he made little progress in promoting his position. In the meantime, Edward House stood in for Wilson at the conference. When Wilson returned, he was appalled by some of the compromises House had made in his absence.

On February 19, a French anarchist attempted to assassinate Clemenceau, shooting at his car as Clemenceau was on his way to a meeting. Clemenceau survived, but a bullet was lodged in his chest for the rest of his life. After a week of recuperation, Clemenceau returned to the negotiations.

⧐ The Council of Four ⧏

The Council of Ten worked slowly, with debates over contentious issues frequently becoming deadlocked. In mid-March, the Council of Ten was superseded by a more informal Council of Four, made up of Wilson, Clemenceau, Lloyd George, and Orlando. The Council of Four met more than 200 times in about six weeks. Most of its sessions were held in Wilson's private study, often with only the four leaders and a translator present.

Orlando spoke no English and took little interest in matters that did not affect Italy. Therefore, most of the key decisions of the conference were made by the "Big Three": Wilson, Clemenceau, and Lloyd George.

ANARCHIST SHOOTS PREMIER CLEMENCEAU, INFLICTING DEEP WOUND IN SHOULDER; PATIENT IS DOING WELL, PICHON SAYS

Premier Lloyd George Summoned Hastily to Paris; King George Sends Message to Premier Clemenceau

...Company
Times
...ily Chronicle's Parlia-

...ris today, (Thursday,)
...s received in Downing
...ive in the view of the
...Clemenceau's enforced

...on Clemenceau, says:
...ad reason to fear that
...re of the allied leaders
...most extensive precau-
...f all the great countries
...ir peace delegates."
...is finding its way into

...ing of Clemenceau was
...occurred, and he kept
...ascertain the Premier's

...ssage to Premier Clem-

...attack on you this morn-
...re not serious and that,

WOULD-BE MURDERER SEIZED

Fires Seven Shots at Premier as He Starts in Auto for Conference.

BEATEN BY ANGRY CROWD

Chauffeur and Police Guard Beside Him Are Slightly Wounded by Bullets.

PRISONER BOASTS OF DEED

"Wished Man Who Was Preparing for Another War to Disappear," He Says.

As covered on the front page of this February 20, 1919, edition of the New York Times, Clemenceau's would-be assassin, Emile Cottin, was captured and beaten by an angry crowd. Cottin became angry at Clemenceau (inset) after witnessing municipal guards firing on striking workers at a war factory a year earlier. For his crime, Cottin was sentenced to the death penalty. However, Clemenceau asked for leniency, recommending instead that Cottin serve eight years in jail.

Two contentious issues caused the most heated debates among the Council of Four. They disagreed on the question of reparations—how should the damage of the war be assessed in monetary terms? How much should they require Germany to pay in compensation? The other point of contention concerned the national claims on German and Austro-Hungarian territory. France demanded control of certain slices of German territory. Italy wanted the Austro-Hungarian territory

A LOST OPPORTUNITY FOR PEACE IN VIETNAM

During the Paris Peace Conference, a young Vietnamese waiter named Nguyen That Thanh attempted to attract the attention of Wilson, Clemenceau, and Lloyd George. He wanted to show them his plan for ending the French colonial exploitation of Vietnam. However, none of the Big Three would listen. Frustrated, Nguyen began writing articles about Indochina for the magazine *Populaire*. His work attracted the attention of the French Socialist Party, whose leaders encouraged him to enter politics. He returned to Vietnam in 1941, changed his name to Ho Chi Minh, and declared Vietnam's independence from France. The struggle that followed was only the beginning of a series of conflicts that eventually led to the United States involvement in the Vietnam War.

The future Ho Chi Minh attends a conference of the French Socialist Party in December 1920 in Tours, France, a year after unsuccessfully petitioning France to introduce reforms in colonial Vietnam at the Paris Peace Conference.

secretly promised to it by Britain during the war, as well as the city of Fiume. On March 28, Clemenceau walked out of a discussion on French territorial claims. According to Mee, that afternoon, Wilson said to curious American delegates, "I do not know whether I shall see Monsieur Clemenceau again. I do not know whether he will return to the meeting this afternoon. In fact, I do not know whether the peace conference will continue. Monsieur Clemenceau called me a pro-German." They eventually compromised and the meetings resumed.

On April 3, Wilson suffered a violent bout of influenza. He lay ill for three days. Some people believe that Wilson never completely recovered his health. When he was well enough to get up, he announced that his patience had run out. He threatened to ready his ship, the *George Washington*, and return to the United States. Once again, a compromise kept the negotiations running.

Orlando withdrew from discussions on April 21, in protest of the council's refusal to cede Italy the city of Fiume. The conference continued without him, and the Italians finally returned to Paris on May 7. They arrived too late to change any of the provisions in the final draft of the treaty.

Fait à Versailles, le vingt-huit juin mil neuf cent dix-neuf, en un seul exemplaire qui restera déposé dans les archives du Gou-vernement de la République fran-çaise et dont les expéditions authen-

Done at Versailles, the twenty-eighth day of june, one thousand nine hundred and nineteen, in a ngle copy which will remain deposited in the archives of the French Republic, and of which

3

Terms of the Versailles Treaty

On April 28, the 160 members of the German delegation arrived in Versailles, a small city close to Paris. The treaty would be signed at the historic Palace of Versailles. The German delegates settled down in their hotel and waited for the Allies to present the treaty. A week later, they were still waiting. Count Ulrich von Brockdorff-Rantzau, German foreign minister and head of the delegation, wondered if the Allies meant the delay as a punishment.

In fact, the Allies had not yet finalized the treaty. On May 6, they were still working on the last points. A summary of the treaty was read out loud in French during the final plenary session, but few of the delegates understood what was being said. None of the Allies had a chance to review the entire document until it was ready to be handed to the Germans. In the middle of the night on May 6, messengers delivered copies of the final version to the most important delegates of the conference. On May 7, the treaty was presented to the German delegation.

The treaty was a massive 200 pages, a total of 75,000 words. It consisted of 440 articles divided into fifteen parts.

This oil painting by Sir William Orpen portrays the signing of the Treaty of Versailles in the Hall of Mirrors at the Palace of Versailles on June 28, 1919. In the forefront of the painting, the German delegate appears slumped in his chair.

∾ Part I — The Covenant of the League of Nations ∾

The first section of the Treaty of Versailles was the Covenant of the League of Nations. It opened with a statement of its purpose: "The high contracting parties, [in] order to promote international co-operation and to achieve international peace and security by the acceptance of obligations not to resort to

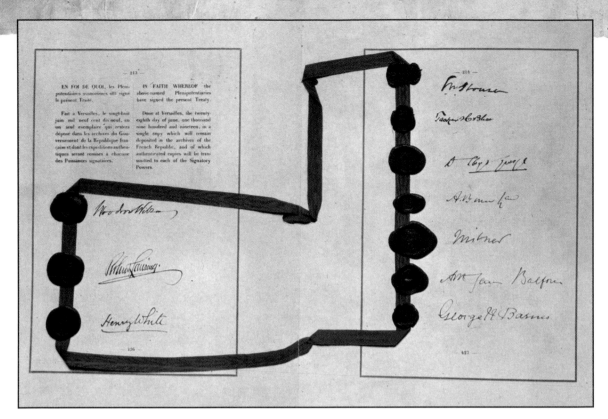

These are the first two signature pages of the Treaty of Versailles, bearing the signatures of the five U.S. delegates, led by Woodrow Wilson, and the five British delegates. Although Germany's two delegates were the first to sign the treaty, their signatures appear last on the final signature page. Refer to page 53 for a partial transcription of the treaty.

war . . . agree to this Covenant of the League of Nations." It consisted of twenty-six articles that described the organization and responsibilities of the League. Article 8 called for the reduction of national armaments. Article 10 stated that League members would help preserve all other members from external aggression. This proved a controversial point when Wilson submitted the Treaty of Versailles to the U.S. Senate. Articles 12 through 14 described the League's system of settling disputes between nations, from arbitration to the consequence of starting a war. Article 22 addressed the League's administration of the mandate system.

∽ Parts II and III—Territorial Dispositions ∽

Ninety articles of the treaty dealt with the new national borders. Germany lost more than 10 percent of its area in the territorial settlement.

Some of the hottest debate among the Big Three focused on French demands for the German territories of the Rhineland and the Saar River valley. Some French politicians called for France to annex the Rhineland. Clemenceau wanted the Rhineland to be detached from Germany and established as a neutral republic. It would serve as a buffer between France and Germany. Lloyd George and Wilson both resisted this plan. They finally agreed that the Rhineland would remain in German hands, but that it would be a demilitarized zone. The Americans and British guaranteed that they would take action against any German military activity in the Rhineland. They also agreed that Allied troops would occupy the Rhineland for fifteen years.

France claimed rights to the coal-rich Saar River valley on the grounds that the Germans had deliberately destroyed French coal mines during the war. Clemenceau sought permanent ownership of the mines in the Saar valley. Under the final compromise, France was given the rights to the mines for fifteen years. Afterward, a plebiscite, or vote, would be taken: the inhabitants would vote on whether to revert the land back to Germany. (In 1935, the Saar valley inhabitants did choose to return to Germany.) France also regained Alsace-Lorraine, historically French territory that Germany had seized during nineteenth-century wars with France.

Belgium was granted the districts of Moresnet, Eupen, and Malmedy. Denmark regained the province of Schleswig, which Germany had annexed in the nineteenth century.

Wilson remained faithful to the principle of national self-determination expressed in the Fourteen Points. Ethnic groups should be granted their own sovereign states. But determining the national borders of Poland, a state that had not existed since the late eighteenth century, proved difficult. The eventual settlement granted Poland more than 20,000 square miles (51,800 square km) of territory. The contested port of Danzig, on the border of Poland and Germany, was established as a free city under the League of Nations. Also on the eastern boundary, the city of Memel was ceded to Lithuania, and the Czechoslovak Republic gained a small parcel of territory.

Article 80 stated that "Germany acknowledges and will respect strictly the independence of Austria . . . she agrees that this independence shall be inalienable, except with the consent of the Council of the League of Nations." This effective ban on the union of Germany and Austria ran counter to the doctrine of national self-determination. Germany and Austria shared common German heritage. According to Wilson's principles on self-determination, they should have been permitted to unite into one nation. It was unthinkable to the Allies, however, that Germany should lose a war only to be granted territory in the peace settlement.

⁓ Parts IV–VII ⁓

Part IV addressed "German Rights and Interests Outside of Germany." Article 119 stated that "Germany renounces in

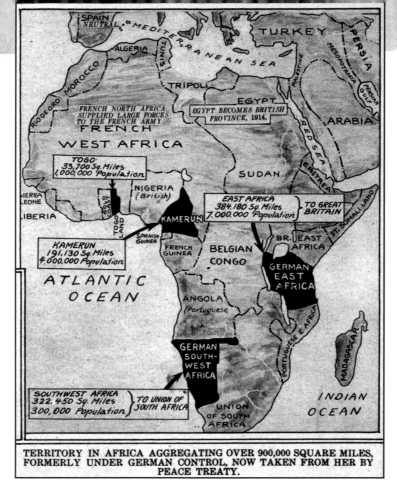

FRENCH NORTH AFRICA SUPPLIED LARGE FORCES TO THE FRENCH ARMY.

EGYPT BECOMES BRITISH PROVINCE, 1914.

TOGO. 33,700 Sq. Miles 1,000,000 Population

EAST AFRICA 384,180 Sq. Miles 7,000,000 Population

TO GREAT BRITAIN

KAMERUN 191,130 Sq. Miles 4,000,000 Population

SOUTHWEST AFRICA 322,450 Sq. Miles 300,000 Population

TO UNION OF SOUTH AFRICA

TERRITORY IN AFRICA AGGREGATING OVER 900,000 SQUARE MILES, FORMERLY UNDER GERMAN CONTROL, NOW TAKEN FROM HER BY PEACE TREATY.

Published in The War of the Nations *in 1919, this map shows the loss of Germany's colonial territories in Africa, as dictated by the Treaty of Versailles. Germany also lost colonial holdings in China and the South Seas.*

favor of the Principal Allied and Associated Powers all her rights and titles over her oversea possessions." The former German colonies would be dealt with under the new League of Nations mandate system. In addition to the colonies, Germany lost "all movable and immovable property" in its former territories. Individuals and corporations would also have to give up their private property.

Part V, "Military, Naval and Air Clauses," provided for German disarmament. It restricted the army to 100,000 men and set limits on stocks of arms, munitions, or any war

German soldiers release poison gas downwind toward Allied soldiers on the battlefield in 1915. It was the first significant use of chemical weapons in a major battle. The major Allies, including the United States, also used chemical weapons during the war.

material. Article 171 prohibited the use of "asphyxiating, poisonous or other gases," chemical weapons that both sides had used during the war with devastating consequences. The German naval fleet was severely restricted, and Germany was prohibited from building any new ships weighing more than 10,000 tons (9,072 metric tons). Submarines were also forbidden. The "air clauses" were even more drastic: Germany was forbidden to have an air force.

Part VI, "Prisoners of War and Graves," addressed the return of prisoners of war and the upkeep of graves of war victims.

The demands of Part VII, "Penalties," infuriated the Germans. It called for the trial of Kaiser Wilhelm II by an international tribunal. Alleged war criminals would also be handed over to the Allies for trial. In 1919, there was no provision in international law for the prosecution of war criminals. The treaty gave no description of the trial procedure or punishment. Opponents argued that the penalty articles were nothing more than a vengeful attempt to fix the blame for the war, and that there was no legal basis for the proposals. In any case, the Netherlands refused to surrender the kaiser to the Allies. The Germans refused to hand over any accused war criminals. In 1925, Field Marshall Paul von Hindenburg, top German military officer and alleged war criminal, was elected president of Germany with no Allied protest.

⚏ Parts VIII and IX — The Reparation and Financial Clauses ⚏

No issue debated at the Paris Peace Conference caused more bitterness than that of reparations. The Allies disagreed on what damages Germany should be held accountable for and how much Germany could afford to pay. France, which had seen the worst fighting and sustained the most damage, wanted to require stiff reparations to help rebuild. Britain did not want the payments to be so steep that they would crush the German economy. Wilson argued that reparations should be based on Germany's ability to pay, and that there should be a thirty-year limitation on payments.

When the Big Three could not agree on a reparations figure, Lloyd George suggested a means of resolving the issue. The treaty would not specify an amount. A commission would later assess the war damages. The final figure would take into account damage done to civilians and their property

This aerial photograph of Arras, France, shows the devastation wreaked on the French town during World War I. France suffered the greatest territorial damage during the conflict, a reality that fueled its insistence that Germany should be severely punished.

during the war. Germany would also have to pay for the war pensions of soldiers.

The reparations section opened with Article 231, later known as the "war guilt" clause: "The Allied and Associated Governments affirm and Germany accepts the responsibility of Germany and her allies for causing all the loss and damage to which the Allied and Associated Governments and their nationals have been subjected as a consequence of the war imposed upon them by the aggression of Germany and her allies." The "war guilt" clause was an official acceptance of responsibility for the war. It sparked more German resentment than any other section of the treaty.

Part IX, "The Financial Clauses," set out in great detail and technical language various rules concerning Germany's obligation to pay reparations.

⁓ Parts X–XV ⁓

Part X, "Economic Clauses," addressed Germany's commercial relations with the rest of the world. In the section on debts, the treaty specified that the Allies could confiscate the private property of German citizens outside of Germany. It would be considered part of German reparation payments.

THE TREATIES OF THE GREAT WAR

The Treaty of Versailles was only one among a handful of treaties negotiated between the Allies and the various Central Powers after World War I. The Russians made a separate peace with Germany under the Treaty of Brest-Litovsk in 1918, in which Russia agreed to extensive territorial losses. Under Germany's armistice with the Allies, the Treaty of Brest-Litovsk was annulled. The Paris Peace Conference produced a number of other treaties besides the Treaty of Versailles. The Allies negotiated the Treaty of St. Germain with Austria, the Treaty of Neuilly with Bulgaria (which had aligned itself with the Central Powers), the Treaty of Trianon with Hungary, and the Treaty of Sevres with the Ottoman Empire. The Treaty of Sevres was later renegotiated as the Treaty of Lausanne and signed with Turkey. These various treaties were named for the locations around Paris at which they were signed.

Part XI, "Aerial Navigation," allowed Allied aircraft to fly over and land in Germany until 1923. Part XII, "Ports, Waterways and Railways," dealt mainly with technical details of international transportation and trade.

Part XIII, "Labor," established an international labor organization to work with the League of Nations. It aimed to improve the working conditions of workers across the world by, for example, "the regulation of the hours of work, including the establishment of a maximum working day and week . . . the prevention of unemployment, the provision of an adequate living wage . . . the protection of children, young persons and women, [and] provision for old age and injury."

Part XIV, "Guarantees," provided for Allied military occupation of the Rhineland. It also required that German troops evacuate territory beyond the newly established national borders.

Part XV was entitled "Miscellaneous Provisions." Among other things, it called for German recognition of certain courts and several other treaties.

Fait a Versailles, le vingt-huit
uin mil neuf cent dix neuf, en
n seul exemplaire qui restera
éposé dans les archives du Gou-
ernement de la République fran-
aise et dont les expeditions authen-

Done at Versailles, the twenty-
eighth day of june, one thousand
nine hundred and nineteen, in a
single copy which will remain
deposited in the archives of the
French Republic, and of which

4

The Failure of the Peace

On May 7, the German delegation returned to its hotel to pore over the treaty. Twenty translators quickly worked on a rough German translation. The delegates were horrified by what they viewed as extremely harsh terms. They began referring to the treaty as a diktat, or a dictated peace.

The German delegates began drafting "observations" on the terms of the treaty, mostly protests. The Allies drafted responses to their concerns, mostly rebuttals. Brockdorff-Rantzau declared that under the terms of the Treaty of Versailles, Germany would not even have the resources to revive its industry, much less pay reparations. Back in Germany, crowds gathered around the American military mission to protest Wilson's hypocrisy. In their opinion, Wilson had broken his promise to base the treaty on the Fourteen Points.

On May 29, Brockdorff-Rantzau presented the Allies with a counterproposal to the Treaty of Versailles. The Germans would keep most of their empire and territory. They would pay a small amount of reparations. Germany and

Several members of the German peace delegation meet informally in a park outside their quarters at the Trianon Palace Hotel in Versailles, France, to discuss the terms of the Treaty of Versailles, which was, in essence, forced on Germany. The delegates were excluded from the actual treaty negotiations and were given only two weeks to accept it. The Allies threatened to invade Germany if it did not sign the treaty.

Austria would be united into one nation. As quoted in *The End of Order: Versailles, 1919*, Lloyd George commented on the German proposals:

> The Germans allege that where the principles laid down in the Fourteen Points work in favor of the Allies, they have been applied in preparing the peace terms, but where they work in favor of Germany, some other principles have been introduced and acted upon—military strategy or economics, etc. Of course there may be some ground for that argument.

German Peace Delegation.
    Translation.   Versailles, May 13, 1919.

To His Excellency Mr. Clemenceau:

In accordance with my communication of May 9th of this year, I have the honor to present to your Excellency the report of the Economic Commission charged with the study of the effect of the Peace Terms on the situation of the German population.

"During the last two generations, Germany has been transformed from an agricultural state to an industrial state. While an agricultural State, Germany could nourish forty million inhabitants.

As an industrial State, it can assure the nourishment of a population of sixty-seven million. In 1913, the importation of goods amounted in round figures to twelve million tons. Before the war, a total of fifteen million persons found an e

This is the official U.S. translation of Germany's counterproposal to the Treaty of Versailles. In it, the chief German delegate, Count Ulrich von Brockdorff-Rantzau (inset), protested the treaty's harsh terms, calling it the "death sentence of many millions of German, men, women and children." See page 54 for a partial transcription of the letter.

The Allies formally rejected most of Germany's objections. They made only a few small concessions. Upper Silesia, a region originally ceded to Poland, would instead be submitted to a plebiscite. The Germans would be given a longer span of time to reduce the size of their army.

On June 19, the German delegation returned to Germany. Brockdorff-Rantzau recommended against signing the treaty. In particular, the delegates unanimously objected to the "war guilt" clause. The deadlocked German government could not come to a decision on whether to sign the treaty.

Gustav Bauer, the German chancellor, sent word to the Allies that the Germans would sign if the "war guilt" clause was deleted. The Big Three rejected the request and gave Germany a twenty-four-hour ultimatum. The war would resume if Germany did not come to a decision. After a great deal of debate and turmoil within the government, Germany accepted the terms of the treaty on June 22.

The treaty was signed on June 28 at the Palace of Versailles. The ceremony took place in the opulent Hall of Mirrors. Dr. Hermann Müller and Dr. Johannes Bell attended to sign on behalf of Germany. Afterward, booming cannons saluted the occasion and the waiting crowds broke into cheers of celebration.

Reaction to the Treaty

Almost nobody was satisfied with the final treaty, even before it was signed. The sections had been drafted by committee, with little consultation between committees. Taken alone, none of the terms were unduly harsh. When put together, however, the cumulative result was a crushingly severe treaty.

One of the British delegates was a young economics expert named John Maynard Keynes. In 1920, he published *The Economic Consequences of the Peace*, a stinging attack on the Treaty of Versailles. The work was so influential that it swayed public policy in Britain, and Keynes became internationally known. He reiterated his criticisms in a 1920 magazine article: "In the first place, this treaty ignores the economic solidarity of Europe, and by aiming at the destruction of the economic life of Germany it threatens the health and prosperity of the

This political cartoon shows Henry Cabot Lodge escorting a battered figure representing the Treaty of Versailles from a room labeled "Operating Room, Senate Committee on Foreign Relations." The Senate committee offered many amendments to the treaty, which President Wilson refused to accept. The Senate eventually rejected the treaty on November 19, 1919.

Allies themselves. In the second place, by making demands the execution of which is in the literal sense impossible, it stultifies itself and leaves Europe more unsettled than it found it." Keynes particularly objected to the stiff reparation demands. Today, Keynes is recognized as one of the leading economists of the twentieth century.

In the United States, the treaty faced opposition on different grounds. Although Wilson had already signed it, the Senate had to ratify it before it could obligate the United States. The chairman of the Senate Committee on Foreign Relations was Senator Henry Cabot Lodge of Massachusetts. There was a personal and political enmity between Wilson and Lodge.

Some senators opposed the treaty because they believed in an isolationist foreign policy. They opposed American interference in international affairs and would not endorse American membership in the League of Nations. Most senators, including Lodge, took a more moderate position. Lodge was willing to ratify the Treaty of Versailles, but he wrote fourteen proposed amendments known as the "Lodge reservations." His reservations focused on the Covenant of the League of Nations. "No doubt many excellent and patriotic people see a coming fulfillment of noble ideals in the words, 'league for peace,'" he stated in a 1919 speech to the Senate. "We all respect and share these aspirations and desires, but some of us see no hope, but rather defeat, for them in this murky covenant . . . We would not have our politics distracted and embittered by the dissensions of other lands." Wilson refused to compromise. In declining health, he went on a whirlwind tour of the United States to drum up support for the Treaty of Versailles and the League of Nations. Nevertheless, the Senate failed to ratify the treaty. The United States eventually negotiated a separate peace with Germany.

Clemenceau also faced protests in France over the terms of the treaty. The French considered the Treaty of Versailles too lenient. "This is not peace, it is an armistice for twenty years," declared French field marshall Ferdinand Foch at the Versailles signing ceremony, as quoted in *Voices from the Great War*. With the Senate's failure to ratify the treaty, the United States reneged on Wilson's promise to come to France's aid against German aggression. In response, Britain also retracted its pledge to support France militarily. After all of Clemenceau's efforts, France was left with no guarantee of security for its border with Germany.

⁓ The Road to World War II ⁓

History books frequently criticize the flawed Treaty of Versailles as a key cause of the instability in Europe that led to World War II. Some historians refute this view, pointing out that no peace settlement would have been able to prevent the postwar crises. The Allies came to Paris with conflicting aims, and they were all dissatisfied with some aspects of the Treaty of Versailles. Germany would have resented any treaty dictated by the Allies, even one with more lenient terms. Four empires had been replaced by a multitude of unstable, sometimes warring, successor states. The statesmen in Paris could not have anticipated the extent of the economic and political chaos of the 1920s and early 1930s—for example, the Great Depression and the violent spread of Communism and other antidemocratic systems of governance.

The Treaty of Versailles might have been more of a success if the Allies had consistently enforced its terms. Part of the difficulty of this lay in the treaty itself. Considering its length and detail, there were very few provisions in the Treaty of Versailles for the enforcement of its terms. The major

THE "NOVEMBER CRIMINALS"

In order to drum up support for their political causes, German nationalists exploited the "stabbed in the back" myth. They claimed that Germany had not actually lost World War I. The army could have pushed on to defeat the Allies. Instead, they had been "stabbed in the back" when the government of the new German Republic signed the armistice. Many Germans believed this version of events and reviled the "November criminals" in power. In 1921, two German nationalists assassinated Matthias Erzberger, the former head of the German armistice commission.

powers gradually adopted a policy of appeasement toward Germany. Within a few years, the Allies did not even attempt to rigorously enforce German cooperation. Desperate to avoid another war as brutal as World War I, they granted Germany concessions in return for promises of peace.

In April 1921, the Reparation Commission assessed the amount owed by Germany at $32 billion. Germany reluctantly began making payments but soon defaulted. In 1923, France reacted by sending troops to occupy the German Ruhr Valley. Germany resisted by slowing industrial output. This caused an economic crisis. The value of the German mark plummeted, and the French franc dropped 25 percent in value. The United States intervened, calling on the banker Charles Dawes to resolve the reparations issue and the declining economic situation. A financial triangle resulted: the United States loaned money to Germany, Germany paid reparations to France and Britain, and France and Britain paid their war debts to the United States. Altogether, Germany paid only about $8.7 billion in reparations, while receiving about $8 billion in loans that it never repaid. France withdrew from the Ruhr Valley in 1924. Afterward, France was much more cautious about taking direct action against Germany.

The Germans were bitter about being forced to take responsibility for the war in the "war guilt" clause, and they resented the loss of German territory. In their view, World War I had been caused by the actions of a number of European countries, especially Russia, Serbia, and France. They blamed reparations for the unstable economic situation. The German people lost faith in the Democratic government of the German Republic, turning instead to extremist

Delegates from forty-one countries attend the first session of the League of Nations' general assembly in the Hall of Reformation in Geneva, Switzerland, on November 18, 1920. President Woodrow Wilson convened the assembly.

movements such as Adolf Hitler's National Socialist (Nazi) Party. The Nazis used German resentment of the Versailles Treaty to their advantage. Hitler railed against the terms in his speech titled "The Treaty of Versailles," which he delivered repeatedly to enthusiastic crowds.

The League of Nations was officially established on January 10, 1920, with its headquarters in Geneva, Switzerland. During the 1920s, it was successful in arbitrating minor disputes between nations. The League faltered during the 1930s, when it could not deal effectively with German and Italian aggression. (In 1945, it was succeeded by the newly organized United Nations.)

The League failed in its goal of international arms reduction. A 1932 to 1934 disarmament conference ended

German forces march across the Cologne Bridge as they invaded the previously demilitarized Rhineland in March 1936. This reoccupation of the Rhineland was a clear violation of the Treaty of Versailles.

in deadlock, and Germany subsequently demanded the right to rearm. If the Allies reneged on their commitment to disarmament, German leaders claimed, they had no authority to restrict Germany's armaments. In 1935, Hitler, who became Germany's leader two years earlier, informed Europe that Germany already had an air force and was planning to build up an army.

In 1936, armed German troops marched into the Rhineland, which the Treaty of Versailles had declared a demilitarized zone. France and Britain, which had resumed their prewar rivalry, took no action against Germany. The United States had distanced itself from political affairs in Europe after the Paris Peace Conference. With its march into the Rhineland, Germany threw off the last of the shackles of the Treaty of Versailles.

Timeline

June 28, 1914   The Archduke Francis Ferdinand is assassinated by Serbian nationalist Gavrilo Princip.

July 28– August 4, 1914   The major powers of Europe begin the hostilities of World War I.

November 7, 1916   Woodrow Wilson is elected to a second term as U.S. president.

January 31, 1917   Germany resumes unrestricted submarine warfare.

April 2, 1917   Wilson asks U.S. Congress to declare war on Germany.

January 8, 1918   Wilson delivers his Fourteen Points speech to Congress.

March 3, 1918   Russia signs the Treaty of Brest-Litovsk with the Central Powers.

October 4, 1918   Germany requests an armistice based on Wilson's Fourteen Points.

November 5, 1918   The Republican Party gains control of the U.S. Senate.

November 11, 1918   Germany and the Allies sign an armistice.

January 18, 1919 The Paris Peace Conference begins.

May 7, 1919 The Treaty of Versailles is presented to the German delegation.

June 28, 1919 Germany and the Allies sign the Treaty of Versailles.

January 10, 1920 The Treaty of Versailles and the League of Nations come into effect.

March 19, 1920 The Senate fails to ratify the Treaty of Versailles in the final vote.

Primary Source Transcriptions

Page 32: Excerpt from the Treaty of Versailles

Transcription

THE COVENANT OF THE LEAGUE OF NATIONS.
THE HIGH CONTRACTING PARTIES, In order to promote international co-operation and to achieve international peace and security by the acceptance of obligations not to resort to war by the prescription of open, just and honorable relations between nations by the firm establishment of the understandings of international law as the actual rule of conduct among Governments, and by the maintenance of justice and a scrupulous respect for all treaty obligations in the dealings of organized peoples with one another Agree to this Covenant of the League of Nations . . .

ARTICLE 42
Germany is forbidden to maintain or construct any fortifications either on the left bank of the Rhine or on the right bank to the west of a line drawn 50 kilometers to the East of the Rhine.

ARTICLE 45
As compensation for the destruction of the coal-mines in the north of France and as part payment towards the total reparation due from Germany for the damage resulting from the war, Germany cedes to France in full and absolute possession, with exclusive rights of exploitation, unencumbered and free from all debts and charges of any kind, the coal-mines situated in the Saar Basin as defined in Article 48.

ARTICLE 190
No submarines are to be included. All other warships, except where there is provision to the contrary in the present Treaty, must be placed in reserve or devoted to commercial purposes. . .

ARTICLE 231
The Allied and Associated Governments affirm and Germany accepts the responsibility of Germany and her allies for causing all the loss and damage to which the Allied and Associated Governments and their nationals have been subjected as a consequence of the war imposed upon them by the aggression of Germany and her allies. . .

ARTICLE 232
The Allied and Associated Governments, however, require, and Germany undertakes, that she will make compensation for all damage done to the civilian population of the Allied and Associated Powers and to

their property during the period of the belligerency of each as an Allied or Associated Power against Germany by such aggression by land, by sea and from the air. . .

ARTICLE 428

As a guarantee for the execution of the present Treaty by Germany, the German territory situated to the west of the Rhine, together with the bridgeheads, will be occupied by Allied and Associated troops for a period of fifteen years from the coming into force of the present Treaty.

Page 43: Leader of the German Peace Delegation Count von Brockdorff-Rantzau's Letter to Paris Peace Conference President Georges Clemenceau on the Subject of Peace Terms, May 1919

Mr. President:

I have the honour to transmit to you herewith the observations of the German delegation on the draft treaty of peace.

We came to Versailles in the expectation of receiving a peace proposal based on the agreed principles. We were firmly resolved to do everything in our power with a view of fulfilling the grave obligations which we had undertaken. We hoped for the peace of justice which had been promised to us.

We were aghast when we read in documents the demands made upon us, the victorious violence of our enemies. The more deeply we penetrate into the spirit of this treaty, the more convinced we become of the impossibility of carrying it out. The exactions of this treaty are more than the German people can bear.

Although the exaction of the cost of the war has been expressly renounced, yet Germany, thus cut in pieces and weakened, must declare herself ready in principle to bear all the war expenses of her enemies, which would exceed many times over the total amount of German State and private assets.

Meanwhile her enemies demand, in excess of the agreed conditions, reparation for damage suffered by their civil population, and in this connection Germany must also go bail for her allies. The sum to be paid is to be fixed by our enemies unilaterally, and to admit of subsequent modification and increase. No limit is fixed, save the capacity of the German people for payment, determined not by their standard of life, but solely by their capacity to meet the demands of their enemies by their labour. The German people would thus be condemned to perpetual slave labour.

In spite of the exorbitant demands, the reconstruction of our economic life is at the same time rendered impossible. We must surrender our merchant fleet. We are to renounce all foreign securities. We are to hand over to our enemies our property in all German enterprises abroad, even in the countries of our allies. . .

Germany knows that she must make sacrifices in order to attain peace. Germany knows that she has, by agreement, undertaken to make these sacrifices, and will go in this matter to the utmost limits of her capacity.

Glossary

Allies The group of countries that fought against the Central Powers during World War I.

anarchist One who believes that society should exist in complete freedom with no government, and may advocate the use of violence to overthrow the established order.

annex To incorporate within the domain of a state.

appeasement The buying off of an aggressor, often by granting concessions.

arbitration The resolution of a dispute by a third party.

armaments Military forces.

armistice A temporary truce between two opponents.

autonomy Self-government.

Central Powers The group of countries consisting of Germany, Austria-Hungary, Bulgaria, and Turkey that fought against the Allies during World War I.

covenant A formal agreement.

czarist Pertaining to the czars, the rulers of Russia until the 1917 Russian Revolution.

default To fail to meet a financial obligation.

delegate A representative to a conference.

demilitarized Prohibited from being used for military purposes.

entente A loose pact of understanding among nations providing for a common course of action.

escalate To increase in intensity or scope.

horrific Causing great shock or distaste.

isolationist Pertaining to a national policy of abstaining from alliances and other international relations.

mandate A territory supervised by the League of Nations and put under the direct administration of another country that would act as its guardian.

mobilize To assemble and prepare military forces for war.

neutrality Refusal to side with any power during a war.

plebiscite A vote by the entire electorate on a proposal, often on a government or ruler.

plenary Fully attended, such as by the members of a conference.

ratify To formally approve.

reparation The payment of damages, especially compensation made by a defeated nation for damages as a result of hostilities.

stultify To make ineffective.

tribunal A court of law.

ultimatum A final demand.

For More Information

The Great War Society
P.O. Box 18585
Stanford, CA 94309
Web site: http://www.worldwar1.com/tgws

Liberty Memorial Museum and Monument
100 West 26th Street
Kansas City, MO 64108-4616
(816) 784-1918
Web site: http://www.libertymemorialmuseum.org/index.aspx

Woodrow Wilson Presidential Library Foundation
18-24 North Coalter Street
Staunton, VA 24402-0024
(888) 496-6376
Web site: http://www.woodrowwilson.org

WEB SITES

Due to the changing nature of Internet links, the Rosen
Publishing Group, Inc., has developed an online list of Web
sites related to the subject of this book. This site is updated
regularly. Please use this link to access the list:

http://www.rosenlinks.com/psat/trve

Fait à Versailles, le vingt-huit juin mil neuf cent dix neuf, en un seul exemplaire qui restera déposé dans les archives du Gouvernement de la République française et dont les expéditions authen-

Done at Versailles, the twenty eighth day of june, one thousand nine hundred and nineteen, in single copy which will remain deposited in the archives of the French Republic, and of which

For Further Reading

Bosco, Antoinette and Peter I. Bosco. *World War I*. New York, NY: Facts on File, 2003.

Coetzee, Frans, and Marilyn Shevin-Coetzee. *World War I: A History in Documents*. New York, NY: Oxford University Press, 2002.

Grey, Paul. *Germany 1918–1945*. New York, NY: Cambridge University Press, 1997.

Jacobs, David. *An American Conscience: Woodrow Wilson's Search for Peace*. New York, NY: Harper & Row, 1973.

Spencer, William. *Germany Then and Now*. New York, NY: Franklin Watts, 1994.

Bibliography

Allied Governments. "The Allies' Conditional Acceptance of the Fourteen Points." From *Foreign Relations of the United States*, Washington, D.C., 1918, Supplement I, 468–469. Retrieved September 8, 2004 (http://www.lib.byu.edu/~rdh/wwi/1918/allies14.html).

The Avalon Project at Yale Law School. "The Versailles Treaty June 28, 1919." Retrieved September 8, 2004 (http://www.yale.edu/lawweb/avalon/imt/menu.htm).

Bailey, Thomas A. *Woodrow Wilson and the Lost Peace*. Chicago, IL: Quadrangle Books, 1963.

Dudley, William, ed. *World War I: Opposing Viewpoints*. San Diego, CA: Greenhaven Press, 1998.

Gilbert, Martin. *The First World War: A Complete History*. New York, NY: Henry Holt and Company, 1994.

Henig, Ruth. *Versailles and After, 1919–1933*. New York, NY: Routledge, 1995.

Lederer, Ivo J., ed. *The Versailles Settlement—Was It Foredoomed to Failure?* Boston, MA: D. C. Heath and Company, 1960.

Mee, Charles L., Jr. *The End of Order: Versailles, 1919*. New York, NY: E. P. Dutton, 1980.

Murphy, Donald J., ed. *World War I*. San Diego, CA: Greenhaven Press, Inc., 2002.

Sharp, Alan. *The Versailles Settlement: Peacemaking in Paris, 1919.*
New York, NY: St. Martin's Press, 1991.

Taylor, A. J. P. *The First World War: An Illustrated History.* New
York, NY: Perigee Books, 1972.

Vansittart, Perter. *Voices from the Great War.* New York, NY:
Franklin Watts, 1981.

Wilson, Woodrow. "President Woodrow Wilson's Fourteen
Points." Speech Before the United States Congress, January 8,
1918. The World War I Document Archive. Retrieved
September 8, 2004 (http://www.lib.byu.edu/~rdh/wwi/
1918/14points.html).

Fait à Versailles, le vingt-huit min neuf cent dix-neuf, en n seul exemplaire 'qui restera posé dans les archives du Gou- ernement de la République fran aise et dont les expeditions authen-

Done at Versailles, the twenty- eighth day of june, one thousand nine hundred and nineteen, in a single copy which will remain deposited in the archives of the French Republic, and of which

Primary Source Image List

Fait a Versailles, le vingt-huit
juin mil neuf cent dix-neuf, en
un seul exemplaire qui restera
déposé dans les archives du Gou-
vernement de la République fran-
çaise et dont les expeditions authen-

Done at Versailles, the twenty-
eighth day of june, one thousand
nine hundred and nineteen, in
single copy which will remain
deposited in the archives of the
French Republic, and of which

Index

ABOUT THE AUTHOR

Corona Brezina is a writer and researcher who lives in Chicago, Illinois. A graduate of Oberlin College and Conservatory, she has written more than a dozen books, mostly focusing on the histories and cultures of various countries around the world. She came to this project with a keen interest in international relations, and was fascinated by the intense political negotiations that took place at the Paris Peace Conference.

PHOTO CREDITS

Designer: Evelyn Horovicz; Editor: Wayne Anderson
Photo Researcher: Jeffrey Wendt